I0418415

Prophetic Seasons – Twelve Months of Divine Declarations
written by Sylvia Richardson
1st Edition © 2026 by Sylvia Richardson
ISBN: 979-8-218-91600-8

Scripture quotations taken from the KING JAMES VERSION (KJV): public domain.

To book Apostle Richardson for a speaking engagement, personal prayer, or to order books by bulk contact Apostle at: Srrichardson.email@gmail.com

PROPHETIC SEASONS

Twelve Months of Divine Declarations

TABLE OF CONTENTS

TABLE OF CONTENTS

INTRODUCTION —

HOW TO USE THIS DEVOTIONAL

There are moments in a believer's life when God calls us to slow down, listen closely, and walk in step with His divine rhythm. This devotional was birthed for such a time. It is not meant to be rushed through or skimmed over. It is a journey of twelve prophetic impartations, each one carrying the breath, weight, and timing of Heaven.

You will read one declaration each month. Sit with it. Pray through it. Speak it aloud. Let the Word of the Lord settle into your spirit and shape your days. These prophetic messages are not simply to be read — they are to be received, declared, and activated. As you meditate on each month's word, expect the Holy Spirit to highlight phrases, stir your faith, and reveal instructions for your personal walk.

The structure of this devotional is intentional. Twelve is not a random number. In Scripture, twelve represents authority, government, order, and divine establishment. There were twelve tribes of Israel, twelve apostles, twelve gates in the New Jerusalem. Twelve is the number God uses when He is setting things in place, aligning His people, and establishing His Kingdom order in the earth.

So as you journey through these twelve months, understand this:

God is establishing something in you.

He is bringing order to what has been scattered.

He is aligning what has been out of place.

He is governing your steps with precision and purpose.

Approach each month with expectation. Read slowly. Listen deeply. Declare boldly. Let these prophetic words become the voice behind your voice as you walk into the fullness of what God has prepared for you this year.

This is not just a devotional. This is a year of divine alignment, authority, and prophetic establishment. Walk through it with faith, and watch God unfold His perfect order in your life.

January –

A Season of Unprecedented Change

"When the time is right, I, the Lord, will make it happen." - Isaiah 60:22

*I*n this pivotal season, we enter a time unlike any other—a season where the ordinary gives way to the extraordinary. As the world faces challenges and transformations on every front, God calls His people to stand firm, trust in His greater plan, and prepare for history-making events. The journey ahead is not about routine or tradition, but about witnessing God's power to expose, renew, and restore. With a spirit of repentance and unwavering hope, we are invited to believe for breakthroughs beyond imagination and to be vessels for a fresh harvest. Step into these greatest days with expectation, for the Lord is making all things new.

❧ God says, it may seem like it's over, but nothing is over until I say so. When you put your trust in me, God says, things are not over like you suppose. It's just completing its last task so it can move on to you. So, it's not over. It's just about to begin, and now it is to begin. And greater it will begin.

❧ My people are going to start to live on a whole new level, both in the spirit and in your natural lives. You can prosper even as your soul prospers.

❧ God says the big exposures are being uncovered. The big evils. I will continue to strip down to the bare-naked bottoms. I will pull down, uncover, and expose the very past history to the very recent history.

❧ God says, and this enemy that you see and have seen before, you will see no more.

❧ God says I must take away, I must expose, before I replenish with my good will for my good people.

❧ God says some of my faithful will become millionaires overnight. Some will be healed in just one second. There will be God-connected happenings in biblical proportions.

❧ Go back and read the stories of what I did for my people in the Old Covenant. and then consider how much more I will do for you in this dispensation. I will do for you that that no man could ever do. And I'll give you peace and joy to join hands to make it complete. For I will complete things I began in you.

❧ God says you are coming into your now time for time itself has been completed and the seeds sown have multiplied spread out and is in full bloom for the harvest is right.

❧ God says you will begin to see this this year and pick up all that you need from seed you have harvested and all seeds still lying dormant. I'm commanding them to spring up speedily because time has had its day.

❧ So seed harvest will be your portion. As I am causing all things to work for you and not the other way around.

❧ I am causing the earth to yield to my people. As first it yielded for Adam before his fall.

❧ God says before Adam fell, the earth yielded to Adam. After the fall, Adam had to yield to the earth.

❧ But now that the second Adam, my son Christ, has redeemed all back to himself, the time has finally come where I am causing this earth to yield back to my people.

✤ God says, command the earth and the earth must respond to you once again.

✤ God says, your voice and my voice must sound the same. As you say what I have already said over you, the voice inside the voice will cause things to move in your favor.

✤ With a blast of the voice of the trumpet, blow out of your mouths that which I have spoken. And whatever you speak, it will respond.

✤ God says many have been feeling defeated. Some have even longed for their journey to end. But remember, there is no defeat in me. So, tell that spirit that it's defeated and not my people. For I have desired to get all out of my people that I have placed in you before you left your heavenly abode.

✤ So, I intend for my people to fulfill your earthly mission. So, when you do return, all will have been accomplished. As did I send my son, and he accomplished it all. All that was asked of him, it was finished.

❧ So, look to Jesus, the author and the finisher of your faith. When you feel like life is too hard. Look to the finished work of the cross and call on your helper, the Holy Spirit, and he will guide you out of and into that place of where I'm directing you.

❧ God says you do have help. Just call on him.

❧ God says don't look for a feeling, But look for the answers to the prayers prayed over you. They will come. Not in a feeling, but in a manifested blessing that you won't have room enough to contain. A spillover of blessings.... All of a sudden, they will begin to chase you down.

❧ Some will say, as Moses said that, that is enough. Don't bring any more because we have more than enough.

෴ God says I'm also expanding your heart's desire to believe me for the greatest not the small or the mediocre but the big and the over-the-top best of who I am and what I am capable of doing for my faithful.

෴ I can do exceedingly abundantly above all you ask or think and above all others that say that they can do.

෴ God says, as I have said before, this is not business as usual, but business unusual.

෴ I'm setting the world stage up for some of the greatest history making events ever seen and my people will benefit from it.

෴ So don't give up now, for you are embarking on some of the greatest days that history has recorded.

෴ And when I expose even more, you will begin to see why I had to allow so much time to go by, because I intend to completely drain the swamp until it is bone dry. From the pulpits to the governments and to the homes in between, because my bride needs to be without spot or wrinkle.

❧ So come to me with a repentant heart to first make yourselves clean and pray for a full harvest with no crop failure, and I will make all things new concerning you, says the Lord of hosts.

FEBRUARY –

THE DAYS OF NOAH'S NEW

"...men who understood the times and knew what Israel should do." - 1 Chronicles 12:32

We are living in a moment where spiritual clarity is no longer optional — it is essential. The times resemble the days of Noah, not in destruction, but in divine transition. God is exposing deception, cleansing nations, and positioning His people for a fresh beginning. This is a season to listen closely, to discern the times, and to align our thoughts with His thoughts. The word that follows is a call to awaken, to stand firm, and to step boldly into the new ground God is revealing.

🕊 God says, don't get weary in well-doing. Hope against hope and endure to your end.

🕊 God says, this spirit of deception is still among many. I have placed Holy Spirit for my people to see the lies and deceit in others that are dressed up as sweet and kind, yet they are lies and heartache.

🕊 God says, it's time for my people to discern the times and the seasons. For you are now living in the days of Noah. But the time of Noah's new. When he and his family stepped out of the ark on dry and new ground. Where Noah built his altar to worship and thank God for the new land.

🕊 God says, to the receding of the waters, and on to the new.

🕊 God says, this is where you are. You have and some are landing on your new. Your new land, your new worship, your new health, your new wealth, and your new relationships.

❧ Some say that the days of Noah refer to the end. yes, but this is not that time. It's the time of the new and not yet the end. It's the time of the settling of the waters, the gracing of your children, the godly decisions, the right decisions that you will now make. A second chance at life. The ending of the old and the beginning of the new.

❧ So this time, think godly. Think and act with godly wisdom. Destroy the old and embrace the new beginnings.

❧ God says, as you put on the mind of Christ, you will begin to think like him. Think only possible, for all things are possible to them that believe.

❧ But the only way to turn all things possible is for you to exchange your old way of thinking for God's way of thinking.

❧ God says, take off those old grave clothes because you are not dying. You are living.

And now in the Zoe way of living. The God life, for you do, after all, belong to me.

🕊 God says, I'm giving you all things, all things to my family. Your inheritance is yours while you yet live on earth.

🕊 God says, you are making history in this time. You are a part of it. The many things going on in this earth today, you are a part of. As you pray, you are making changes and the history of your world for the better.

🕊 God says, change in the spirit nor in the natural in your ways. God says the filth of the swamp of the nations was so deep that I had to do and to do it my way. So, this will never come up again or it will be like when Saul was told to kill off everyone and everything in the camp. But he didn't and eventually they rose up again to fight against my people.

❧ God says, so trust me in the process and in your nations and in your personal lives, for I am God and I have full knowledge of both where good and where evil lies. I see behind every rock and every rocky heart.

❧ Soon you will see the good overtake the evil and peace will reign in your cities and nations and your lives as you're walking into your reign you will walk into king Solomon's place where peace and plenty was the rule of the day.

❧ But first, we must finish off the rule of his father, King David, the mighty man of conquering wars, the king that had no fear, the king that won every evil battle.

❧ God says, but remember, there was always a war and an uproar before the win, because there can be no win without a war, No battles, no wins, no fights, no conquering.

ﻬ But in these battles, I am fighting for you, with you, and because of you. Many of these battles, you can't even see. Many are in the spirit where I do my best fighting.

ﻬ God says, the things the enemy had planned for you, my people, you will never see, because I've already sent my angel army to finish the fight in the heavenlies.

ﻬ So, you keep fighting the good fight of faith, and I'll take care of my part, says the Lord of hosts.

MARCH –

THE REMNANT RISING

"Whoever says to this mountain, 'Be taken up and thrown into the sea,' and does not doubt in his heart... it will be done for him." - Mark 11:23

*T*his prophetic word calls us to rise above the mountain experiences that once held us, to speak with the authority God has placed within us, and to step boldly into the kingdom assignments prepared for this hour. It is a reminder that we are not crushed to be broken but crushed to reveal the God who lives within us. For those who have sown faithfully, endured quietly, and trusted deeply, the time of harvest is drawing near.

❧ God says, there is an intensity coming. As I am moving, so is the evil one. But I will always cause you to triumph. Victory is always yours. My people will see the banners written over your heads. So don't ever let go of your God. This is a supernatural era that you are living in. Your season that you call fall; you will see a wrapping up of many things in your lives.

❧ You will see me tying up loose ends. You will see me finishing off and starting new things. For my people have been around this mountain long enough. Now you're digging trenches. No more digging trenches, says the Lord.

❧ It's time to carve yourselves out of that mountain experience and use it for your good. It's time to speak what remains of the mountain and tell it to move.

❧ God says you have the authority. You rule over your mountains. For I see my image in you. I see my likeness in you.

❧ So, rule as I rule and keep on becoming paths of righteousness. For you have been set aside for the higher calling in Christ Jesus.

❧ Take that narrow road less traveled. That road of quietness. That road of aloneness. Not loneliness, but the state of being alone, where disappointment no longer disappoints because you know that you have your God. Where the state of being alone just means that you have been set apart to do the greater will of God.

❧ God says, I've made nature even for your examples. The fish of the sea, some are bottom feeders. Then there are the great whites. There are tiny fish that just swim in a school together, never leaving nor drifting apart. Then there's the great whale, the king of the sea, where he dominates the waters as year after year he migrates to new and different parts of the ocean. Where the sea is calling, where the deep calls unto thee. A place where only you can go to hear my voice, my heart, and my intentions for the soul of my faithful.

☙ God says, it's kingdom business from now on. It's all about the king and his business. So, get the blueprints. So, you, my people, can colonize and set in order my kingdom on your earth. Where heaven will begin to look like your earth and earth my kingdom, and where love, peace, and joy are the rules of the day.

☙ God says, I have set aside a remnant of people that have gone the extra mile, that have given their very last and their very best at my command. A people that have gone through hell to get to heaven A people unshaken by the world and the things of the world. A people where heartache and disappointment can no longer hurt them. A people that react only to the good that comes out of the bad. A people carved out of stone heating in the fire and undrowned by the waters of life's trials.

◆ They can now lay their heads down on a pillar of fire and not be burned, only to get up again, loving my image and likeness. These things have made them to be God-like.

◆ God says life is here to make you strong, to make you a strong people, and not to weaken but to mature and to grow and to challenge the me in you to come out and to shine so others can see your God in this earth.

◆ You are here to reveal me. You have been crushed to prove that I do exist. You have been issued an issue to prove the God in you is an overcomer and a devil slayer, able to do and accomplish more than you ever thought possible.

இ God says hurt is always for your good when I'm in it because I cause all things to work together for your good. To improve and enhance your lives I know the plans and the paths that I have for you, my remnant and I know just what weight you can bear.

இ So, if you're feeling the weight of the pressures of life, moment to moment, just know what I am doing. I know just how strong I've made you and I won't allow you to carry a hundred-pound weight where you're only a 50-pound level. I'll give it to you in small measures yet pressing you daily towards the mark of higher calling.

இ God says, and you will be pleased with the measure of endurance you have and are achieving. Achieving. You will look back to see how strong you have become because you have allowed me to strengthen you. You will look back and thank me for the closed doors as well as the open doors.

God says no more letting the lots of your future doors in and leaving the lots where you have found them. And if I allow them in your door of opportunity, it's only because they should be there. Not just because they wanted to tag along.

God says things aren't always what they appear to be when you are looking with your natural eyes.

God says see like the great eagle and use your three set of eyelids and see beyond what's in your view. See beyond the dark clouds and see your silver lining for the silver lining is your place of there. If you can see it, you can believe me for it. And as sure as I am God, you will receive it.

God says, you have planted seed. Now sit back and know it's harvest time. And if your seed, soil, and watering were good, so shall your harvest be. The birthing of your

harvest is upon you, says the Lord Most
High.

THE RISE OF THE EAGLE PEOPLE

"But those who wait on the Lord shall renew their strength; they shall mount up with wings like eagles..." - Isaiah 40:31

There are seasons when God calls His people higher—into clarity, maturity, and spiritual altitude that few ever reach. Like eagles rising on unseen currents, the faithful are lifted into realms where vision sharpens, strength renews, and purpose becomes unmistakably clear. This is a time of blooming, of ripened fruit, of stepping into the fullness of what God has been cultivating for years. The word that follows speaks to elevation, readiness, and the divine timing that positions God's people for open doors, restored streams, and supernatural opportunity.

ಈ God says, look to the eagles, for they fly at an atmosphere unknown to bird kingdom.

ಈ God says, there's a newness and a brightness my people are beginning to feel. You are beginning to sense the blooming in your spirit.

ಈ God says, it's been budding in you for years. The blooming process has been slow, but it has been sure. It has been constant. There is a fruit living inside that is becoming ripe that many are about to pick from.

ಈ God says, my people are becoming trees of righteousness where you are bearing much fruit. The great eagle, you, my people, are likened to. For you have beat your wings against the clefts of the rocks. You hid in caves where the bomb of Gilead has healed you. You have sharpened your beaks, and now you're ready to do it again. You're ready for the lift, that greater wind, that stronger wind, to blow you up even higher.

☙ God says, for there is no ending in me, and no searching for end of me. Just when you think you've got it, I will turn again to breathe on you once again so that you can see and know even more who I am.

☙ God says there will never be an ending of who I am on this side of heaven or on the heaven to come. I am the beginning and I am the end. But there is no beginning or ending in me, I always was and I always will be.

☙ God says the newness is finally here. I've been waiting for you to grow up into it.

☙ God says you, my faithful, look so good in your new college level. You have put away the milk and now it's the meat. You have put away childish things. That era is over. Some will be fed in small portions, but there's my elect that will be fed out of the professor.

❧ Sir/Maam, you will teach the class because you have been fed the entire meat. Because you have already been taking my word little by little, year after year, line upon line, precept upon precept. And you think that you're not ready. You think that you're ill-equipped.

❧ But I am your equalizer, your stabilizer, your voice behind the voice. I am your rotator. When I'm rotating out of them that have been there in that space where you will now take your turn, like the turnstile that comes one in and the other goes out, rotation for everything.

❧ There are a time and a season, the entire old Babylonian system has fallen. That slave system is in rotation, and I am replacing that slave system with my new and better way of life, where all will be free, and I, and only I, will be your God.

God says that I'm bringing my people out from among the Egyptian army and you are now crossing your Red Seas. Your Red Seas lives are upon you. You are getting ready to go to the other side. You are free and you will stay free.

God says, begin to see that great opportunity right before you, right before your eyes. You won't need to look for opportunity. I will set it before you. For I have set before you an open door that no man nor devil will be able to shut.

God says, I am paying my faithful back for your faithfulness. I am the door opener, and I am bringing in God connections that you've never thought were possible. For I am the God of the impossible, the God of all flesh.

Is there anything too hard for me? I say no. And as you say no, the impossible will become possible.

In a millisecond, God says, I'm opening up the four streams again that were in the Garden of Eden. I am undamning all that has been stopped up, the flow of the provision and the things that have been trashed, that have trashed the four streams and have kept them from revealing to my people. I am creating a new river and new riverbanks that will hold so much that it can only spill over into the lives of others.

God says I have set up the dominoes and now my finger has finally touched them and they are falling right one after another right into place. Not one will fall off. Perfect timing and perfect precision they will fall for I am the God of all, and you will soon see why the wait was so long, yet so necessary.

God says, stay in sync with my precision timing, for it will take you there and what you will need to know and everything that you need will meet you there and your right set appointed time will be full. There will be no lack of anything. You and it will arrive right on time in the fullness of time with nothing missing where there will be joy unspeakable and full of my glory.

◈ God says you have been diligent. You have done the hard work. And now you will enter into this next portion of your lives with ease and work accomplished written over your heads, says the Lord of hosts.

MAY –

HELP IS HERE

"And I will ask the Father, and he will give you another Helper, to be with you forever." - John 14:16

In times of pressure, delay, and shaking, it can feel as though God has stepped back and left us to figure things out on our own. Yet Heaven's reality is the exact opposite: help has never left. In this prophetic word, the Lord reminds His people that the Holy Spirit is still present, still moving, and still orchestrating deliverance, justice, and breakthrough behind the scenes. Cycles are shifting, Pharaoh's systems are collapsing, and a great roundup of the faithful is underway as God prepares His people to become a pure, glorious dwelling place for His presence.

❧ God says help is here, your helper the Holy Ghost, has never left you God says but the cycles haven't been here for my glory and my goodness towards my people collided but there will be and already is happening a colliding of my miracle power to my people like you've not seen in this dispensation

❧ God says I showed Moses my ways and the acts to the people. There will be a showing and a knowing of my goodness to them that stayed the course. To them that seek my face, my heart, and not just my hand.

❧ God says to them that don't live in Lodabar, but rather, to them that walk and live in the spirit are going to see every promise open up to you suddenly.

❧ God says the days of the impossible turning possible are here. For I am the one that made it all. And there is nothing impossible with me.

◈ God says some have closed their eyes and turned their heads away from me, because you didn't get what you wanted when you wanted it. You grew weary in well-doing. You lost hope and faith.

◈ But God says you too have a place in the winner's circle. So, get back on your cycle of trusting me again. And I will cycle back around to you. Just pick your faith self-up and keep on believing. Get up one more time and watch me shine in your life.

◈ God says, and then stand still and see the salvation of the Lord once again. Because I am blanketing this world with my grace and my glory. And it's receiving time. Time to pull out your best blanket and wrap up that that you will manifest because you have pushed through, believed through, and now you will deliver what you have been carrying.

❧ God says, you are my greatest creation. Do you not think that I would let you go or let you down? I keep my promises to a thousand generations and it's time again for me to deliver my promises.

❧ God says the wait is over. You're in the delivery room in the position to receive your rewards of your faithfulness.

❧ God says I'm shutting down all of Pharaoh's systems one by one. Now watch as the Hammons are hung. As I expose every swamp rat that has been trying, one more last attempt against my people. But this too will fail because I am fighting against the evils that you can't see. And the banner written over your heads are, my people have won by the mighty hand of God.

❧ God says there will be peace and a freedom in the land as in the days of Solomon's reign.

God says we are moving from the David battles to Solomon's reign. My people will build the tabernacle. Only this tabernacle will be on the inside of you. You will make a great dwelling place for me, says the Lord. For you are my tabernacle, and I will dwell in your pure, clean, undefiled bodies as you make room for me in yourselves to do the mighty miracles.

God says give me permission to abide and I will show the unsaved world what it looks like when the creator of heaven and earth can do in and through a willing and obedient body.

God says this world is quickly moving into the great prosperous change. The change you have been waiting for. The change you have believed and prayed for is here. Step by step, line upon line, here a little, there a little, change has been creeping up, and suddenly you will look up and see, I have done all this for you and in this world for you to enjoy.

❧ God says, I told you I'm coming back for a glorious church without spot or wrinkle. So, shall you be able to enjoy all that I will do for you before I come for you?

❧ God says, I am rounding up my people from the four corners of the earth. I spew out the lukewarm and tighten up the hot. They are called by my name. I'm calling from the deep places. Deep is calling too deep.

❧ God says, my spirit is calling on the innermost parts of your spirit to do my will, so your joy will be full. The great roundup is taking place for my people and because of my people. Steering and branding of my sheep is here. There is a great movement under your feet, a shaking that will change the very course of your lives. Only feel the rumble and then begin to turn from your shallow waters into the

deeper part of me, that when the greater
shaking comes, you will not be moved, yet
you will be changed for the greater good,
says the Lord of hosts.

THE ERA OF MIRACLES AND OPEN DOORS

"Not by might, nor by power, but by my Spirit, says the Lord of hosts." - Zechariah 4:6

There are moments in history when God steps into the affairs of His people with unmistakable power—moments when human strength is no longer the engine of progress, and divine intervention becomes the only explanation. This prophetic word speaks to such a moment. It announces a season where signs point to wonders, wonders unfold into miracles, and miracles reveal the faithfulness of a God who remembers His covenant. For those who have endured the wilderness, trusted through the night, and held fast to His promises, the dawn of accelerated fulfillment is breaking open.

❧ God says, you have stepped over into your time of my signs pointing to wonders, and the wonders will be my miracles.

❧ God says, this is the time that I am showing my ways and my acts to them that have believed in me over the years. There is much need for what I am doing because my people can't do it on their own. What I am doing and what I am going to do for my faithful and my faith field. Only I can do, not AI and not humankind, without the help of my mighty right hand.

❧ God says again, it's not by your power nor by your might, but it will be by my spirit. My handing down the gavel of every movement. I am giving out the yeses and the amens. I am releasing the new table that will be set before you. God says the enemy is playing checkers, but you're on the chessboard and my people are not playing. You mean to win and you will, and you are winning. God says that the fight is fixed because the plea for life and death have already been won when my son fulfilled his earthly duties. He's won a great family. He's brought back and bought back with his holy blood and redeemed mankind.

🙷 God says, now the Abraham doors are released to have been open. You have begun to see the connection after connection and will see connection after connection as the doors begin to swing wide open for my people. As opportunity began to chase you down.

🙷 God says it's finally your time, for you have come out of Egypt and now it's time for your land that will flow with milk, honey, silver, and gold.

🙷 God says the golden doors are opening. Where whichever one you stand before will hold your goods Your time of rewarding is here in the measure that your heart and your hands have given.

God says, for I have resurrected your promises that you thought you would never see in this life. For they weren't dead, they were like Lazarus, only sleeping, to awake at the right set time, so all would know that only God could have done it.

God says, step aside and watch me do my great wonders in your lives. Watch as you believe and praise me for my people will be in awe of my miracles.

God says there will be a sudden change, sudden abruptness, sudden movement, complete about faces. For the rivers have been dammed up for years, but to ever-flowing streams in your wilderness. Provision met on every side, access granted, door openings, and the enjoyment of the works of your hands. Because your hands have applauded me, and your heart has trusted in me in the wilderness. Watch as you pray. I will close hospitals as I heal my people.

❧ God says it will be all over in the morning. For the night for my sons and daughters have passed and you have now moved into your mourning. Just because it's still dark does not mean that it is not morning. For the breaking of the dawn is just ahead of you. So, rejoice in the dark because it's morning. The darkness of the morning leads you to the light, and the light of morning is illuminating your treasures.

❧ God says, watch as before you call, I will come with the answers. While you are still speaking, I have already heard. It's the speeding up of all things, the remembering of my promises to my covenant people. It's the dominion and the power and the subduing and taking all things that belong to you. It's the tearing down of the old and the building up of the new with a stronger and righteous foundation driven by and powered by the Holy Ghost himself.

◈ God says every time you look up, it will be win-win in every situation that you allow me to touch. Give me permission and watch me go to work on your behalf. It's the rehearsal and the reversal of the hurricane, blowing out all that is sucked up and placing it back to where it belongs, only with a fresh wind of my greatness.

◈ God says, observe to do my commandments so it will be well with you. For my burdens are easy and my yoke is light. All you need to do is lean in on me and I will work in this era. I will do miracles and you will do the obeying. So together we can see the winning.

◈ God says there will be rapid growth and things that will hurt your hearts before will be like water rolling off a duck's bat because of your growth. The tears cried in the past will be only that they have watered your growth.

God says there will be times now when you want to cry but you will remember your past and know that if I brought you through that, that this is no reason or season to cry about it in your now. For I am faithful and I want my people to be faithful to me knowing that if the door is shut, I have the ability to open it and make it work in your favor. For this is the era that I am turning every no into a yes, every red light into green. So, move now with confidence and authority, for I am the same God today, yesterday, and forevermore, says the Lord of hosts.

JULY -

THE WELLS OF THE FAITHFUL

"Therefore, with joy you will draw water from the wells of salvation." - Isaiah 12:3

J uly opens with a divine shift in spiritual supply. The Lord is redirecting His people from shallow, inconsistent sources into deep, established wells of His provision. This month carries the theme of exchange — small for great, lack for abundance, dryness for overflow. Heaven is emphasizing maturity, stewardship, and readiness as God separates what is true from what only appears true. July is a month where the faithful begin to recognize that the resources of God are not random but intentional, and that He is positioning His people to receive, to teach, and to carry greater mantles for the sake of His kingdom.

● God says the voice of the Lord is a force.

● God says the little wells are changing places.

● The big wells are finding their place in the lives of my faithful. Wells filled with the living water of God, filled with everything you need and, yes, desire. For your desires come from me.

● God says, I am drying up the small wells, and I am rerouting them to the deeper wells of my resources, where my faithful will have plenty.

● God says, I am ridding the greedy of always being takers.

● Even when they don't need it, they store up and never give up anything to my people, storing up riches and goods for themselves only while my people go and lack.

● God says to them that are led by the Spirit are the sons of God, not them that are led by their own fleshly desires and the things of the world.

🐚 God says the silver and the gold are mine. The precious things of this earth and money answers all things.

🐚 God says, I'm giving the money to my people so it can answer your things, and you can put your hearts on me without the thought of things.

🐚 God says, not just to give to them, but to teach them to fish. And they in turn can teach others to live.

🐚 God says you are walking into the fullness of times as heaven is touching your earthly timing.

🐚 So, readiness is imperative, both in your spirit and in your natural. God's great promises are coming to pass. God's glory is coming this time not to destroy but to reveal your new and your kingdom living —

your kingdom spouses, your kingdom businesses, your kingdom lifestyles.

◄ᕼ The wheat has grown up, and the tare has grown up with it. And my people and them that are not yet on the threshing floor. And I'm doing the separation. For they have been put on the threshing floor for my separation. I'm shaking out all that doesn't look like me.

◄ᕼ I'm exposing the tare and destroying the purpose of its very existence. And my wheat is emerging as well-grown stalks, mature and ready to feed the billions of souls that are to be mine.

◄ᕼ God says, you have done things in the past, broke. You have done things in the past, broken. But this time I am blessing you to look like Joseph at his time of reigning. You will have enough to give out and to teach out of your blessed hands and your blessed mouths. I will give my faithful a new heart full of compassion for the exchange of your stony heart that was sufficient for your past. But now, as the days have grown more evil, more of your compassion is needed for your new — a compassion for souls.

☙ God says, you won't take the things that people say against you so personal, but you will have compassion for their souls.

☙ God says, entrust with the gifts that I have placed inside of you to steward. For my sake, you will receive another mantle on top of what you have already gotten. There will be no taking of mantles that I have given to you, but you will double up on the ones you already have in order to do my kingdom on the next level of anointing. For those that refuse to pick up their mantle, I will be placing them on the shoulders of them that can steward both.

☙ God says, even them that have gone on, I will allow you to pick up their mantles — the passing of the baton — and run with it to keep my kingdom alive and well.

◆ God says there is a movement in all things, even in your fall, even in my new year movement of building, movement of everything.

◆ There is a time and a season and a purpose to everything under the sun — to culminate into that building and tearing down at the same time, to the planting and the harvesting yet at the same time, to that living and dying yet at the same time, to the sowing and the reaping yet at the same time — because the time of it all has already been realized. You have already put in the time. So now is the time of your seeing what you have put in in time, for both naturally and spiritually.

◆ God says your new days are greater than your old days. The old days have, as some say, are not your good old days, because your greater days are just before you. The latter house is greater than the former house, and life as you used to know it will pale in comparison to what I have in store for my people that have been found faithful to my cause.

❧ God says it's time to rejoice, it's time to celebrate, and it's time to reconcile a nation back to me, as I reconcile a people back to me, and begin to hand out earthly rewards — pressed down, shaken together, and running over, says the Lord of hosts.

AUGUST –

THE GREAT TURNING: WHEN THE END BECOMES THE WIN

"Is anything too hard for the Lord?" —
Jeremiah 32:27

August arrives as a divine pivot — a month where God interrupts the narrative of decline with the announcement of victory. While the world rehearses rumors of collapse, God draws a clear line: doom is not the portion of His people. This is the month where the end of the year becomes the beginning of the win of the year, where what looks like "going down" in the world becomes "coming up" for the faithful.

In this prophetic declaration, God reveals a sweeping reversal: the systems of the wicked crumble while His people rise into the kingdom system — a system marked by joy, peace, equity, and the abundance He has always intended. August becomes the threshold where long-held promises begin to breathe again. The Lord honors a generation that believed through heartbreak, *disappointment, and tears, and now He announces that every tear He has bottled will be shaken into beauty.*

This month carries a commissioning. God calls His people to speak to the dry wells within and around them, commanding them to spring up. He reminds us that age is not a barrier to promise, that Joshua-and-Caleb strength still rests on those who refuse to bow out early, and that long life is not only possible — it is purposeful. August becomes a month of divine reassurance: you will not leave this earth until you have poured out everything, He placed within you.

God affirms the faithful who endured the process, who became towers of hope through seasons of breaking, refining, and stretching. He honors those who leaned on Him alone, stewarding strength not just for themselves but for others who needed their courage. And now, He declares that the best of all times stands directly in front of His people — the "good God era," the season of great reward.

Even as shaking hits the earth, God promises it will be short-lived and turned to the advantage of His people. Light will outrun darkness. Giants will fall for the final time. And victory will once again be written over the heads of those who have remained faithful.

August is not merely another month — it is the divine hinge where everything begins to turn.

❧ God says the end of this year will be the beginning of the win of this year as rumors of doom and gloom come to your world, just know that it's not for my people.

❧ It's the going down and the coming up for the wicked it's going down and its systems and for my people, especially my faithful and obedient, your bringing in the kingdom system, where joy, peace, happiness and equity for all my people will be produced.

❧ God says, for it is finally your time because it's finally my time to show up and to deliver the goods to my people. A generation that has outlived your promises, yet you hoped against hope. You still believed in me in the midst of your heartbreak, your disappointments, and your tears.

❧ God says, as I have bottled them all up, and now I will shake them all up and turn your ashes into beauty.

❧ God says, I'm putting an end to sorrow the sorrow of lifelong pain, and an end to a life of disappointment, and I'm bringing in life and life more abundantly, for that is one of the many promises to my people of hope.

❧ God says, speak to your dry whales and command them to spring up spring up, O whale, spring up, and be the fuel of the water of God.

❧ God says, some have said, how can I believe for the mansion in heaven when I can't see my way on earth?

❧ God says, it's that one reason that I'm coming to you before I come for you, so I can give you all that God's heart desires for you.

୫ God says the angel of death has been passing in the earth, but my people that have been standing in the land of Goshen with the blood of my son on the doorposts of your hearts will not see death for a long time, for I am making my people to live out your lives in order to reproduce that that I've placed in sight of you. You will not die until you have emptied yourselves of the god goodness that I put there.

୫ God says I put things inside of my people when I birthed you out of your mother's womb, and I want all emptied out into the lives of others and into this world, so when you return, you will be empty. You will be complete and full of only my glory, as you will come home with mission accomplished. Some have said in their minds that they are getting older, but where in my word did I say your age must stop you from my promises?

✺ God says, remember Joshua and Caleb. They conquered their mountains and received their promises at a ripe old age and enjoyed many years thereafter.

✺ God says many have been leaving this world at an early age, and it's only because their missions were accomplished early in their lives, and many wanted to come home, so rejoice in your years. It only means that with long life I will satisfy you because you have and are satisfying me.

✺ God says I say again to my faithful only be strong and courageous, for I need you to be there for others to pull through the strong and don't ask me to bring you home because I need your courage to help others come into their place of there.

✺ This is the reason I allowed things to build up in you, so you could help others the weaker ones to get up, and that's why I thank you for your obedient heart and your diligence to keep on going, no matter what.

❧ God says, I've thrashed you through the process, and in the process, I have processed you into becoming that tower of hope to so many others.

❧ God says some have said to me and me alone that you can only lean on me, and it was because I put the strength and the fortitude in you to follow me solely, but are all are not equipped with the strength I've given to others, so thank you for believing and stewarding the strength that I have given to you so others can live.

❧ God says, many have made me proud despite your heart breaks, for it was the breaking of the good heart that enabled the soundness of the god heart, and I thank many of you for taking the hard times in order to achieve the best of times, and the bests of all times, God says, are just in front of you. You have stepped in the land and in the place where good will walk in front of you to make sure that your path is clear to move into your good, your 'good God era', and it's only your portion and no longer the bad God says it's your 'great reward era', and you say I can hardly wait. Well, I can hardly wait to see you with your own eyes, and you will see it with your own eyes.

❧ God says remember that I am the God of all flesh. There is nothing too hard for me, especially after what I will do for you that you will see with your own eyes.

❧ God says, don't worry about what you will see that will seem contrary to what I've said, for it will be a strong shaking before the awakening, but it will be short lived, and I will use it too, for my benefit whatever the devil uses, I will cause it to work in your favor, because light is stronger than the dark, and my words are greater than the voices of darkness. So when the enemy comes in, I will rush in a

flood out of his darkness and destruction
and turn it into the goodness for my people
as you will watch Haman once again hang
on his own gallows and thrash his spear
into his own heart, you will watch giants
not only fall, but die out completely, never
to be seen or heard of again, so rejoice your
redemption to destruction is drawing nigh,
and victory will be written over your heads
once again, says the lord of host,

THE ONE-DAY TURNAROUND: WHEN GOD ANSWERS AT THE SPEED OF THOUGHT

"Before they call, I will answer; while they are yet speaking, I will hear." — Isaiah 65:24

September enters with a divine acceleration — a month where God collapses the distance between prayer and manifestation. This is the season where answers arrive at the speed of thought, where the impossible becomes the expected, and where the faithful begin to witness miracles in forms no generation has ever seen. God announces that this is not the time for conventional outcomes but for supernatural impact, the kind that leaves His people stunned by the undeniable evidence of His hand.

This month marks the reward of patience, obedience, and endurance. What once felt unstoppable will be stopped. What seemed empty will overflow. What looked impossible will bow to the God of all flesh. September becomes the sunrise moment — the "too good to be true" season that proves itself true.

God calls His people out of the dark side of their story and into the bright side of His glory. He reminds us that just as Christ's suffering gave way to joy, our long seasons of heaviness are giving way to the Christ-side of life — the life of the Bride, the life of glory, the life of divine lifting.

This is the month where one day can change everything. Where evening darkness gives way to morning glory. Where the rod of your mouth becomes the instrument of breakthrough. Where Red Seas part again. Where the bottom becomes the top. Where the latter becomes greater than the former.

September is not just a month — it is a divine shift into accelerated answers, supernatural authority, and the dawning of a new era.

God says I will be hearing and answering at the speed of thought, so when before you call, the answer is already there. Don't get afraid because it's prayer-answering time.

God says my people will start to see my miracles take place as this generation has never seen before, but don't look for things to appear in the conventional way, but in the supernatural, impactful way. For I am leaving such a great impact on my people's lives that it will be to you almost unbelievable, but it will be undeniable.

God says for some it's just that time where your patience and your obedience has just paid off, but it's really just my time to stop what seems to be unstoppable, give where it seems there is nothing left, and to do the impossible because I am the God of all flesh and there is nothing too hard for me. Your time of "this is almost too good to be true" is.

coming up with the sunrise. It will be like a fresh cup of coffee on a cold day. It's going to be a wild moment — a "this is just what I needed and asked for, only greater."

God says I didn't put my image and likeness in this world just for tears of constant sadness or mediocrity, but the tears of joy will be mixed into your lives. It's time for balance — from sadness to joy unspeakable. It's time for mediocrity to become more than you could ever imagine. It's time for lack to become your overflow.

God says you've been on the dark side of your lives living, and now it's time to see the bright side of your lives.

God says the dark side of my Son's suffering while on earth was finished after going through His passion, the finished work of the cross, and His bright side is now having a family surrendered to Him. For the joy that was set before Him was

His bride. And now your dark side of life in your world will soon be a thing of your past as you embrace the Christ side of life by joining in with the journey of being His bride.

◈ God says I'm going — I'm going to be the glory and the lifter of your heads. I am your ray of sunshine. I am your bright and your morning star. I am everything you allow me to be. I am getting the job done, and all I need is one day, not ten years.

◈ God says many will see me move on your behalf in one day. And the evening and the morning were the first day, and all creation changed. These will be your stories. The evening will be dark and void, but the morning and one day will be full of my glory for your lives and in your lives. It's time for my faithful to believe me in all walks of life.

◈ God says why bother to pray if you don't believe that I can and will make it happen?

So, start praying for things you think are impossible, so when I bring it to pass, you will know that it was me.

☙ God says there was no power in the rod of Moses unless it was given by me, and there is no power in the rod of your mouths unless given by me. So, use your rods of authority and use the power I've given to you, for life and death is in the power of the tongue. And I give you the power and authority to use it so you can see your Red Seas part right in front of your eyes and the crossing over onto dry and better ground — ground that belongs to you. This will be your portion.

☙ God says this is your time of deliverance and freedom from all that has held you in bondage. This is your time from living on the bottom to living on the top. The end of this year is the beginning of your new, as you're exiting out of your old journey and stepping into your new. Your latter days will be greater than your former days, and the glory of the latter house will be greater than your former. These are the days the apostles of old wanted to look into, so be about my business in a way that only this generation can do. Them of old did just what I instructed them. They walked upright before me, even without Holy Spirit living inside of them. How much more should Holy Spirit-filled people of today move and live, as you have the Greater One on the very inside of you — not just walking alongside of you, but inside your very being. That's just how close I am to my people. I walk both alongside and inside of my people. I am faithful and just to move in a wave of glory from the inside to the outside, for you are my surrendered servants with my power and glory and authority. My signet ring is stamped on the hearts, so move in my authority.

God says for the winds of change have blown in and blown the walls of the Red Sea back once again, as I have recycled back around to the days of the great and notable miracles. Rejoice — the days of joy and abounding once again, for this is a people that has never seen it like this before, says the Lord of Hosts.

THE RISING: FROM THE HARD SIDE TO THE HIGHER SIDE

"He satisfies your years with good things, so that your youth is renewed like the eagle's." — Psalm 103:5

*O*ctober arrives as a month of reversal — a divine turning from the hard side of life to the higher side of destiny. This is the month where God acknowledges the hidden battles, the backwards beginnings, the childhood storms, and the long seasons of endurance that shaped His chosen ones. Many entered the world in trouble, grew up in the lean places, and walked through darkness long before they understood the God who walked with them. Yet even then, eternity tugged at their spirits, marking them for the throne.

Now God declares that the other side of life is opening. The years of surviving are giving way to the years of rising. The hellish seasons are yielding to a little bit of heaven on earth. Strength has been preserved for this moment, and resurrection life begins to break through in both spirit and body. October becomes the month where age loses its power, where youth is renewed, and where the newness of God begins to overshadow the memories of yesterday.

This is a month of reward — not for perfection, but for faithfulness. For trusting in the dark. For enduring fiery trials known only to God. For showing up when it was hard. For believing when it made no sense. God now calls His people to step into opportunity, to see in the spirit, to rise from the ground, and to embrace the limitless life He intended.

October is the invitation to ascend — to rediscover identity, reclaim dominion, and step into the higher life of God. It is the month where the faithful begin to see prosperity, favor, and harvest long promised. The fall months become the gateway to high blessings, and the faithful step into the season prepared for them.

God says many of my chosen have come in this world backwards, and that you came in in the time of trouble. You have been living life on the hard side and the lean side of life, yet you always followed God in the dark. Even when you didn't know that there was a God, you knew of me and followed after me.

You felt eternity in sight of you. You were dripping with heaven's calling on you, able and did survive, and grew through the hardest times, even as a child, yet you knew in your young spirit man that you were destined for the throne.

God says and now you are going to embark on the other side of life.

God says you have been through your hell times on earth, and now it's time for your little bit of heaven on earth. You always somehow knew that your time would come, but it's been so long coming that you began to wonder if you would ever be alive to see it.

❧ God says I have kept you strong and alive for this time. You will see your resurrection of life. You will see your fullness of life.

❧ God says I have been renewing your youth as the eagle without all the old sad memories of yesterday's gone by.

❧ God says I am giving you the new in that my word says behold, to look, to gaze upon. I will make everything new.

❧ God says some even feel it in your bodies and in your mindset — the newness of life, both the God life and in your natural life. Where others seem to be failing, you are being renewed.

❧ God says stop thinking like the world, saying it's an age factor. Age is nothing to me.

◦ Just look at my patriarch Abraham, Job, Joshua, and Caleb. I preserved, renewed their lives, and I am doing the same for my precious elect today.

◦ God says some have come through fiery trials, things only you and I knew about, yet you loved, served, and trusted me. Some even, like Job, said, "Though you allow me to be slain, yet will I trust you." Well, it's time to get in the line of rewards, because I am rewarding your faithfulness for all the years gone by where you trusted the process and knew that I was your hiding place.

◦ God says I am asking my faithful to show up when opportunity arises. Just show up, and I will be your door opener or not. It's time to explore other options. It's time to go forward. It's time to see the world in the spirit. You have seen it in the natural, and now it's time to move to see in the spirit. That will broaden your spirit world — see and believe for the higher life. Don't just stay on the black side of life, not knowing that there's a whole world to see, both in the natural but especially in the spirit. Know that there are no limits to your faith. No, it is no limit of possibilities of life more abundantly.

❧ God says I want my people to live that high life, that God life, to do it God's way, and the sky can have no limits to where I can take you.

❧ God says my faithful have been living too close to the ground, and it's time to rise to the higher, to the deeper depths. And yes, because it's time and because I have made you to have dominion and to subdue and to recover all that belongs to you.

❧ God says how can you say that you are my image bearers and my glory carriers when you are on the ground? It's time to reach the higher in me, because when you find that part of me, you will find that part of you that will make you want to reach for the stars.

❧ God says you are fearfully and wonderfully made — a one of a kind, a look-alike like me, made after to reproduce who I am: to love and to have peace, power, and supernatural ability; able to ascend into the highest far above the enemy's camp; able to step back and see the plans of the enemy and to rise far above them; and well able to reproduce my love to the unsaved.

❧ God says there's yet a harvest of souls to be had for the kingdom, so study to show yourselves approved to go and to gather in the harvests. And as you gather in those that are mine, I will release to you what I have in my heart, my plans, and in my hands for you, because it gives me great pleasure to see the prosperity of my people. And now is your time, especially to my elect, my faithful, for me to pour out my favor, my faithfulness toward you. So,

watch your fall months for high blessings to
start to come to you, says the Lord of
Hosts.

NOVEMBER –

THE LOCKED-IN PROMISE: RESTING WHILE HEAVEN WARS FOR YOU

"Before they call, I will answer; while they are yet speaking, I will hear." — Isaiah 65:24

November enters as a month of divine assurance — a season where God reminds His people that their prayers, decrees, and faith have not been in vain. This is not the month of striving but of resting in the God who fights the battle. The Lord calls His people to breathe in the fragrance of victory, to remember past deliverances, and to trust that the same God who provided water, manna, and quail will once again supply both what is needed and what is desired.

This month carries a profound revelation: your promises are locked in. Heaven has already mobilized angelic armies on your behalf, aligning time, circumstance, and spiritual authority so that what God has ordained cannot slip away, delay, or be stolen. November becomes the month where the believer learns to walk by the Spirit, to trust divine thoughts over natural reasoning, and to step into the authority that has always been theirs.

God calls His people to rise as His remnant — a unified voice of righteousness, a people who decree what Heaven has already spoken. This is the month where spiritual senses sharpen, where authority is reclaimed, and where creation itself waits for the sons and daughters of God to speak order into chaos.

November is not passive. It is the month where rest becomes warfare, where obedience becomes dominion, and where the voice of God through His people becomes the force that reshapes the world.

◆ God says you have been praying, decreeing, and believing, and continue to do so. It's a spiritual war, but you need to remember to enter into my rest because I am the Lord of the fight. Stop and smell the victory of every win, knowing I'm in your battle and I am your battle-axe. When evil or ill winds of trouble seem to blow, remember what I did for you in the past.

◆ God says don't be like the children going through the wilderness wondering if I will do it again, wondering if I will give you water in your dry place, wondering if it's your manna and if it will show up every day. And then I gave you not only what they and you need, but I will give you what you want, and I gave them what they wanted. The quail came up by the nettles.

◆ God says so will it be for my people today if you don't complain, as their complaining made them take the long road home. But if my people today will praise, believe, and take your rest in me, I will take you through your journey with what you need and yes, what you want.

☙ God says for I have said before that before you call, I am already answering. Just as Daniel prayed, I heard his prayer, but I was setting up the angel armies to fight his battles and to answer his prayer. So, continue to pray, and more importantly continue to believe that I have already heard your prayers, and I am sending you your answers at the right set time, in the fullness of their time. So, when your prayers are answered, time will be set in place where your promise cannot escape your hands. They won't be able to go forward in time or escape backwards in time.

☙ God says your promises are locked in.

☙ God says listen to my instructions, as you will hear a word from behind you say, "This is the way, walk ye in it," for I will give you thoughts that are not your own. They will be my thoughts, my ways that will prosper you. So, follow the leading of the Holy Spirit, no matter how strange it may seem to your natural minds. Don't allow your natural thoughts to outweigh your spiritual mind, for the spirit mind knows all things, and I search out all things that pertain to godliness in Christ Jesus.

- God says I have set you in this world, but I make you in this world to show my authority and to live out my image and my likeness by defeating the devil on every hand.

- God says if you only knew the authority that you have, you would rule like I will.

- God says never exchange my yes for the enemy's no when you are the ones that hold the power of life and death in your lives.

❧ God says so if I said yes, then yes is what it is, and you then say yes and rule with your God-given authority.

❧ God says I'm building up and unifying a powerful army, a powerful voice of righteousness, a remnant that will secure my word with their voices. As you say what I have already said, as you decree what I have already decreed in the heavens over your lives.

❧ God says but you must live right. You cannot live on the fence for what I am unveiling. You can't let your mind rule over the mind of Christ.

❧ God says command your spirit senses to take over your natural senses, and you will be able to break down walls, call out unrighteousness, sniff out devils hiding in places, and touch no unclean thing that will not do.

❧ God says all of creation is waiting on the sons of God — you, my faithful — to call this world back into order. Creation is waiting to hear again the voice of God through my people that are called by my name.

❧ God says so use my name, use your authority to co-create with me, to cause this voidness and chaos to stop. Command the wind and the waves once again to obey my will. I want my faithful to be in such relationship with me that when you speak, I hear myself speak, and my words will never return void to me but accomplish on earth that which I will. That will be your portion, says the Lord Most High.

THE DROMEDARIES ARE COMING: HEAVEN'S CARRIERS OF PROVISION AND PROMISE

"Then you shall see and be radiant... the abundance of the sea shall be turned to you; the wealth of the nations shall come to you. A multitude of camels shall cover you... all those from Sheba shall come." — Isaiah 60:5–6

*D*ecember arrives as the grand finale — the month where Heaven's provision, promise, and fulfillment converge. Throughout the year, God has been building His people: strengthening them, refining them, renewing them, and positioning them. Now, in the final month, He unveils the imagery of the dromedaries — Heaven's prophetic symbol of endurance, wealth, resilience, and divine delivery.

In Scripture, dromedaries carried treasure, covenantal gifts, and generational promises across impossible terrain. They survived heat, drought,

*and harsh landscapes, converting their own
reserves into water so the journey never stopped.
God now declares that this same supernatural
endurance and unstoppable provision is being
released over His people. What He has promised is
not fragile. What He has ordained cannot be
delayed. What He has packed onto the backs of
His "dromedary angels" will arrive — through any
weather, any resistance, any season.*

*December becomes the month where God's people
stand at the great gate, waiting for Heaven's
butler to swing the doors wide. It is the month of
finales and suddenlies, where treasures long
promised to begin to manifest — health, wealth,
resources, restoration, and the desires of the
faithful. This is the month where God reminds His
people to come up higher, to abide in the secret
place, and to expect the fullness of the finished
work of the cross.*

*The dromedaries are not a metaphor of hope —
they are a declaration of arrival.*

Heaven is delivering. Provision is moving.

*The year ends not with a whisper, but with a
caravan.*

❧ God says the dromedaries are coming. Why the dromedaries, you ask? God says it's because they can carry the heavy weight and with swiftness. God says they can transport my valuables through the heat of the desert. You can count on them to get the job done. No matter the heat of the desert sun, when nothing else can get it to you, my dromedaries will.

❧ God says they are the creation of me that can and does get the work done. They were and are used for carrying heavy burdens that man cannot, as I am your burden bearer.

❧ God says they are used for converting the fat into water, and I am that living water that never runs dry. Dromedaries are used for riding through the harsh terrain, as I will allow you to ride on the wings of my angels. And the dromedaries are used and associated with carrying great wealth, prosperity, and divine provision with endurance and resilience.

🐪 God says Abraham sent his servant out on his dromedaries to find a wife for Isaac, filled with good treasure. I sent the Queen of Sheba with great treasures to King Solomon on the dromedaries. And God says I am sending my dromedary angels full of heavenly treasures as well as natural treasures to my people, to my covenanted people, to my people of promise. I'm sending the dromedaries with their backs packed full of my goodness and promised treasures.

🐪 God says they will make it through any weather — all heat, snow, or rain.

🐪 God says and if they get tired coming to you on your journey, that fat on their backs will convert into water and they will carry on, making sure they get to you your treasures.

❧ God says the resilience through anything — these animals get the job done, and so will I make sure my people get the job done. And surely, I will get it done with great provisions. I'm getting to you.

❧ God says many will be known as carrying great wealth, being associated with great prosperity because of your great resilience and endurance of life's hard lessons. Yet you endured to your end, and yet you believed that you would get there.

❧ God says you're getting there is closer than you think. It's just a matter of you standing at that great gate waiting for the butler to open the doors wide and to bring my faithful all that the heavenly dromedaries are carrying for you — my people that are called by my name. For there is a place of resemblance to where I abide, in that secret place where there is nothing lacking.

❧ God says so continue to look up higher, to come up higher, to abide in that secret place where all is provided.

❧ God says there are caravans of dromedaries on their way to your homes, carrying all that is for you in this season of finales and suddenlies.

❧ God says some will come with a gift of health on their backs, some with silver, and some with gold. But all will carry your valuables — your whatever you need, and yes, what you want.

❧ God says as a dromedary symbolizes God's great provisions, God's great wealth, God's way of getting through to you anything — so shall it be to you, my people, my faithful, my elect. So, look to the angelic dromedaries. They are on their way, and their backs are full of my treasures that I have for my saints of today.

God says forget not my benefits, for all of the finished work of the cross belongs to you, my people, and is on the way. They are standing at the door waiting for you to believe them in, says the Lord of Hosts.

AUTHOR BIO

Apostle Sylvia Richardson is a seasoned minister of the gospel whose prophetic voice has strengthened, encouraged, and awakened believers for several decades. As an ordained Apostle and Christian Counselor, she carries a unique blend of spiritual authority, pastoral compassion, and prophetic clarity that has shaped her ministry and touched countless lives.

Apostle Sylvia holds a Diplomate Certificate in Christian Counseling from Marketplace University, equipping her to minister with both biblical insight and emotional wisdom. Her counseling work reflects her heart to see God's people healed, restored, and aligned with their divine identity and purpose.

Known for her bold prophetic accuracy and her unwavering commitment to the truth of God's Word, Apostle Sylvia ministers with a distinctive cadence — direct, Spirit-led, and deeply rooted in Scripture. Her teachings and prophetic impartations call believers into maturity, discernment, and a deeper walk with the Holy Spirit. Whether speaking, counseling, or writing, she carries a consistent mandate: to build up the Body of Christ and prepare God's people for the seasons and assignments ahead.

Throughout her years of ministry, she has served as a spiritual mother, mentor, and counselor to many, offering guidance marked by wisdom, compassion, and an unmistakable presence of God. Her prophetic words have brought clarity in times of confusion, strength in seasons of transition, and hope to those navigating spiritual battles.

Apostle Sylvia continues to minister with humility, passion, and a deep love for God's people. Her life and calling reflect her unwavering desire to see believers walk in freedom, strength, and the fullness of their Kingdom purpose.

www.ingramcontent.com/pod-product-compliance
Lightning Source LLC
Chambersburg PA
CBHW070437130626
46553CB00006B/2224